the Gift

The Gift
J.John

Originally published 2006 by Verite CM Ltd.
This revised edition published 2010 by Authentic Media Ltd.

Scripture quotations are taken from the Holy Bible, New International Version.
Copyright © 1973, 1978, 1984 by Biblica. Used by permission of Hodder & Stoughton
Publishers, a member of the Hachette Livre UK Group. All rights reserved.

British Library Cataloguing in Publication Data
A catalogue record for this book is available from the British Library

ISBN: 978-1-86024-726-2

Cover design: Chris Jones
With special thanks to Liza Hoeksma for her editorial expertise.
Photography by Becky Welford   www.beckywelfordphotography.com
With thanks to the May Family for all their help.

Printed and bound in Great Britain by Bell & Bain Ltd, Glasgow

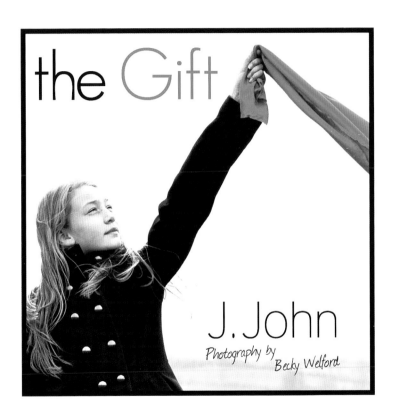

the Gift

J. John

Photography by *Becky Welford*

I love Christmas; it's a time of magical sparkle. I even enjoy the annual tradition of Christmas shopping and present hunting. One comedian commented, 'Christmas is a time when we exchange a whole lot of gifts we really like for a load we don't want.'

We've probably all been in the position of having received that indescribable gift – then been lost for words when we opened it in front of a doting relative. As someone perceptively said, 'Christmas is a season of emotional family ties – especially when you have to wear them.' I see all this as a challenge and adventure – especially when it comes to shopping for my wife Killy.

It hasn't always been easy, though. There has always been plenty to learn. When we got engaged, I remember trying to buy Killy a dress for Christmas. I didn't know her size so the woman serving me asked if she was bigger or smaller than her. What could I say...? Eventually, the shop assistant tried on the dress!

After many years of marriage, however, and many miles spent trawling up and down shopping centres, I have developed four criteria when it comes to buying a gift for Killy. It's more of an art form than a precise science, perhaps, but nevertheless, these four things steer me away from the 'panic buy' and towards something more soulful and meaningful. In the process, my four criteria remind me of the gift God has given each of us.

Two millennia ago, the apostle Paul wrote this: 'Thanks be to God for his indescribable gift!' (2 Corinthians 9:15) or, as one translation puts it, 'a gift too wonderful for words!' What, then, are the four criteria of my gift-buying for my wife Killy at Christmas time?

First, I want to make sure my gift for Killy will be personal – I want to find something that she can really appreciate. These days, I've stopped buying her what I want; after more than a quarter of a century of marriage, I now know what she likes. After all, it can be very disheartening to receive a present that doesn't have that personal touch. One Christmas a friend of mine received a half-empty packet of sausages for Christmas that his mother-in-law had left over from a recent visit!

One of the greatest gifts in life that we can receive – especially at Christmas time – is the revelation and realization that God knows each one of us personally and wants us to know him personally, too. In the Bible, Psalm 139 is a startling and beautiful reminder of this fact:

O LORD, you have searched me and you know me.
You know when I sit and when I rise;
you perceive my thoughts from afar.
You discern my going out and my lying down;
you are familiar with all my ways.

When you stop to think about it – and it's important to do just that – then it's a mind-blowing thought: God knows us intimately. He is not an abstraction or a mystical 'higher power'.

The tiny hand of God

Consider for a moment: have you ever placed your finger inside the hand of a little baby and felt its grip? If a baby tugs at your finger, it also tugs at your heart. Christmas is the powerful grip of a tiny hand reaching from a bed of straw. It is love, tugging our hearts back to God. As the Bible says, God, invisible in his own nature, became visible in ours. Beyond our grasp, he chose to come within our grasp.

And this is the intimately personal nature of Christmas: God gave us his Son for our sake. 'For God so loved the world,' says John's Gospel, 'that he gave his one and only Son, that whoever believes in him shall not perish but have eternal life' (John 3:16).

He loved the world so much that he gave us a life-giving gift of such a personal nature that we couldn't begin to dream such a story or such a gift into being.

In fact, the breadth and depth of God's love is hard to fathom. A young father, whose wife had just died, took his daughter on a cruise to begin the recovery process. As they huddled together on the deck of the ship, the little girl asked her father, 'Daddy, does God love us as much as Mummy did?' At first, the man didn't know quite what to say. But he knew he couldn't side-step the question. Pointing across the water to the distant horizon, he said, 'God's love reaches farther than you can see in that direction.' The man then looked up at the sky, and said, 'God's love is higher than the sky, as well.' Finally, he pointed down at the ocean and reflected, 'It's deeper than the ocean, too.'

After hearing her father speak, the girl responded: 'Oh, just think, Daddy. We're right here in the middle of all that love.' It sometimes takes a child to help us understand the nature of the Father's indescribable gift.

It's life – but not as we know it

However, God's gift to us wasn't a one-off that ended when Jesus died for our sins. The Bible tells us that Jesus rose from the dead three days later, and opened the way for us all to live forever. When he returned to heaven, he sent God's Spirit to live within anyone who would receive him – so that everlasting life (and 'life to the full', as Jesus described it) could begin now, not just when we get to heaven.

In giving us his Spirit, God has drawn us into intimacy with himself; he is with us and has come to live within us. One of Jesus' titles is 'Emmanuel', which translates as 'God with us'. For all who choose to make room for him at the inn of their heart, this Jesus has become a gift that could not be more personal.

2. The Practical Gift

When I buy a gift for Killy, I want it to be personal. But I also want it to be practical.

Most of us end up receiving at least one or two presents each year that are as much use as a chocolate teapot. Sometimes, people will even give a gift to make a point – like the DIY book I received one year!

It reminds me of the woman who once stuck her Christmas wish list to the fridge for her husband to read. She kept it brilliantly simple, asking only for 'something that will make me look slim and beautiful'. When Christmas arrived, she looked forward to opening a package with something gorgeously intimate inside. Instead, she got an exercise bike.

Santa might bring us what we deserve; God, however, delivers something we don't deserve. 'For the wages of sin is death,' says the Bible, 'but the gift of God is eternal life in Christ Jesus our Lord' (Romans 6:23). God's practical gift to us, then, is forgiveness.

19

In the run-up to Christmas, we do lots of tidying, preparing and cleaning – sprucing up our homes, our clothes, even our bodies. Many of us will have a haircut or even go for a manicure to help us look and feel better. But God's gift goes much further than hand-wash.

Jesus is more concerned with what's on the inside. 'Blessed are the pure in heart,' he once said, 'for they will see God' (Matthew 5:8). His practical gift is to cleanse our hearts. This changes us from the inside out, transforming our attitudes and actions.

However, we must want the gift in order to receive it. We need to pray with the writer of Psalm 51, who said, 'Create in me a pure heart, O God, and renew a steadfast spirit within me.' Consider for a moment, how exciting it is to give a personal present that you've put so much thought into, and how crushing it is if the person opens it, and discards it without so much as a look, let alone a 'thank you'.

Are we hungry for what God has to offer? Jesus was born in Bethlehem, which literally means 'the House of Bread'. Later in his life, he spoke about himself in picture language, saying, 'I am the bread of life. He who comes to me will never go hungry, and he who believes in me will never be thirsty' (John 6:35).

Bread satisfies and strengthens, and Jesus came into the world to satisfy and strengthen us all. But this isn't, as we have already seen, a gift to be received passively, end of story. It's practical by its very nature. When we receive Jesus, we also receive his Spirit, which helps us to live a brand new kind of life – with love, joy, peace, gentleness, patience, self-control and humility.

While your past may be stained with regret, with God you are offered a spotless future. But we all need to respond to the gift God has given. A personal, practical gift from God demands an appropriate reaction. In U2's No. 1 single 'Vertigo', Bono sings that God's love is teaching him how to kneel. His response to the gift is one of humility and worship. God can do so much more with you than you can do with yourself.

24

3. The Permanent Gift

So, God's gift is personal: he gave us his Son. And God's gift is practical, because it helps us to cleanse our lives, satisfying and strengthening us. But when I give a gift to Killy, I also want, if possible, to give something permanent: something of lasting value that she will treasure way beyond Christmas Day; something that will not perish.

Sometimes, we can give our children expensive toys, only to find, by the end of Christmas Day, that they prefer to play with the boxes or the wrapping paper. Occasionally, the presents we give them don't even work, or they break before they've had the opportunity to use them properly.

God's gift to us, however, is permanent, not perishable. It won't need to go back to the shop. Remember those immortal words from John's Gospel: 'For God so loved the world that he gave his one and only Son, that whoever believes in him shall not perish but have eternal life'?

I recall explaining to my son, Michael, when he was about three, that if he chose to disobey his mum and me he would have to live with the consequences. 'Daddy,' he said with a terrified look on his face, 'please don't make me live with the consequences. I want to live with you and Mummy.'

But there are consequences if we don't obey those who know better. Imagine one of your children playing on the road. You see a fast car approaching, but you know you can't reach them in time. Running toward them you shout, 'Get out of the road.' It is crucial at that moment that your child trusts you and responds. Are you trying to ruin their fun? No! You are trying to save their life.

Well God, our heavenly Father, knows that we are all in danger. We're at risk of spending eternity separated from him. That's why God sent Jesus – it was to give us the opportunity to go to heaven. 'I tell you the truth,' he said, 'whoever hears my word and believes him who sent me has eternal life and will not be condemned; he has crossed over from death to life' (John 5:24). Life without Christ is a hopeless end, but life with Christ is an endless hope.

GW.5.85 kgs
N.W.5.55 kgs
MEAS.76x28x28 cm
C/No.599

27

4. The Purchased Gift

So, God's gift is personal – he gave us his Son. It is practical, through the cleansing of our hearts. And it is permanent, not perishable. But when I find a gift for Killy, I also like to purchase it before walking out of the shop!

God's gift to us was, likewise, purchased. It didn't come for free – in fact, it came at a huge cost and we should not cheapen it by discarding it lightly. God gave us his only Son. We couldn't save ourselves, so Jesus came to rescue us.

When lifeguards rescue someone who is struggling in the sea, they will swim out to them and tread water. They don't grab onto someone who is drowning. If you try to save someone who's frantically trying to save themselves, they will pull you under. So instead, a lifeguard will wait until the person they are saving has run out of energy. When they've given up struggling, the lifeguard can take hold of them and swim back to shore.

Similarly, if we try to save ourselves, God can't save us. Jesus rescued us by purchasing forgiveness when he died on the cross. The Bible says, 'He is the atoning sacrifice for our sins' (1 John 2:2).

One Christmas, a grandmother could not decide what gift to give her three grandchildren. She decided to simply put a cheque for £20 in each card with the message, 'Buy your own gift'. The cards left in the post but then, to her surprise, the woman found the three cheques under some newspapers – she had forgotten to put them in the envelopes. Her three grandchildren were very perplexed to receive a card, each with the startling message, 'Buy your own gift'.

This is the startling truth of the gospel – Jesus Christ has purchased our redemption. We now have to receive that gift for ourselves, acknowledging that there's nothing more we can do to attain God's forgiveness than accepting it through his Son Jesus. We are saved by having faith in Jesus to rescue us – not by thrashing around trying to stay afloat through doing good works.

God spent everything he had on us. And the gift is one that we shouldn't want to exchange for anything else.

32

For Best Results Follow Maker's Instructions

My heart sinks when I open a Christmas present only to see three little words printed on the top of it: 'Some Assembly Required'. I once read about a man who ordered a tree house for his children. It duly arrived, and the time came for him to assemble it. He laid out all the parts on the floor and began reading the instructions. To his dismay, however, he discovered that, while the instructions for a tree house were there, the parts were for a boat! The next day he sent an angry letter to the company complaining about the mix-up. Back came this reply: 'We are truly sorry for the error and the inconvenience. However, it might cheer you up to remember that somewhere there is a man out on a lake trying to sail your tree house.'

To put something together, you have to have the right instructions. Thankfully, when it comes to our own lives, God has revealed to us the best way to assemble them. Through the Bible's wise instruction and the guidance of the Holy Spirit, we are free to accept God's gift of life, and make the most of it.

A Free Gift? You'd Better Believe It!

God doesn't force himself upon anyone, however. He offers his gift, but he won't make you take it. He's already reached out to us through the life and death of his Son. It's up to us to make the next move.

It's amazingly simple; we can accept God's gift by simply believing in it. The word 'believe' dictates the action on our part. To believe means to 'commit' or 'to rely and depend upon'. It means putting your trust or faith in something or someone.

God's gift is universal – he freely gives it to 'the world' and it's available to all – but each of us must believe for ourselves that Jesus lived among us, died and rose again. Jesus floods our life with meaning, joy and renewal – but only by our personal invitation. As the Bible says, 'to all who received him, to those who believed in his name, he gave the right to become children of God' (John 1:12).

One Christmas, I was given gift vouchers for a department store. As you can imagine, I was very excited. Foolishly, however, I left them on my desk for months, and, as with most gift certificates,

they had an expiry date. Thankfully, I made it just in time! Gift vouchers are only of any value if we redeem them. Likewise, God wants us to redeem his gift to us by believing and receiving Christ.

Experience the Love!

A professor of English literature once wrote a book on the subject of love. The only problem was that he had never been in love himself. When he took the manuscript to a proof-reader to have it prepared for publication, she turned out to be a very lovely woman. When their eyes met, something happened to the professor that was not in his book. With love rushing in to fill his heart, he became more joyful in the following five minutes than he had been in the previous fifty years when love lived in his head alone.

Like the professor, we will never experience the love that God wants to show us unless we meet him and look into his eyes.

Receiving the Gift

In 1983, I found myself standing before a minister who asked me a question: 'Will you take this woman to be your lawfully wedded wife?' I'm no fool, so I said, 'Yes.' He then turned to my wonderful bride, Killy, and asked her likewise, whether she would accept the man standing before her. To which, I am glad to say, she also responded with a 'Yes'. At that moment, through the willingness we expressed to commit ourselves to one another, Killy and I entered into a special, loving relationship that has forever changed our lives.

The Bible tells us that 'God demonstrates his own love for us in this: While we were still sinners, Christ died for us' (Romans 5:8). Just over 2,000 years ago, God gave an answer to the question of whether or not he was willing to enter into a loving relationship with us. By coming to Earth in the person of Jesus Christ, he gave us a resounding 'Yes!' Now, he puts the question to each of us. And if we answer, 'Yes, I am willing to believe and receive Jesus Christ,' we, too, will enter a relationship with the God of the universe that will change our lives forever.

At Christmas, when we receive gifts we may not need or want, God offers something of far greater worth that we can't do without. All it takes is to believe and receive the gift yourself: a personal, practical, permanent and purchased gift that is yours, for life.

These famous words were penned by Phillips Brooks in 1867 and became the last verse of the carol 'O little town of Bethlehem':

O holy Child of Bethlehem, descend to us, we pray;
Cast out our sin, and enter in, be born in us today.
We hear the Christmas angels the great glad tidings tell;
O come to us, abide with us, our Lord Emmanuel!

It expresses well what we need to do to receive God's personal, practical, permanent and purchased gift, who is Christ Jesus.

Why not pray this prayer based on Phillips Brooks's words as a way of receiving God's indescribable gift?

O holy Child of Bethlehem, descend to me, I pray;
I turn from sin, please enter in, be born in me today.
I've heard the Christmas message the great glad tidings tell;
Christ come to me, abide with me, O Lord Emmanuel!
Amen.

J.John Christmas Gift Books